BACKYARD KILNS

Steve Mills

Text and Photographs Copyright © 2015 Steve Mills

Illustrations Copyright © 2015 Cameron Kerr. All rights reserved.

ISBN: 1511846453
ISBN-13: 978-1511846455

DEDICATION

For the one that got away

CONTENTS

	Acknowledgments	i
1	Introduction	3
2	History	5
3	Construction	9
4	Door Construction	15
5	Additional Information	21
6	Materials and Tools List	23
7	Plans	25
8	Firing	31
9	Construction Modifications	35
10	Photos	39
11	Additional Reading	49

ACKNOWLEDGMENTS

A number of good friends have had a part in helping me put this together from proof reading to recommending things to put in or take out. So thank you to Lucy, Mike, Nikki, and Wes, and above all to my Wife Kate for being patient!

"BEFORE WE START"

If you are contemplating building a fuel burning kiln, there are several things that you need to take into consideration:

- Where are you going to build it?
- Is it a heavily populated area?
- How close are your neighbours?
- Have you told them about your plans in detail and are they agreeable?
- If it is not your land have you asked the owners permission?
- Do you need planning permission?
- Is it a clean air zone?
- Does what you plan to do contravene any local by-laws?
- Have you checked with the fire department?
- Are you in an area which has dry seasons with a consequent fire risk?

This may all seem basic stuff, but it all needs to be carefully checked out, after all this is something we are enthusiastic about, and a wrong or thoughtless action can create a lot of bad feeling, and potentially wreck anyone else's chances of doing something similar in the future.

Potters are generally very environmentally aware, so the idea of us building a fuel burning kiln, and perhaps creating a fair amount of smoke in the process, makes us vulnerable among other things to the charge of having double standards.

"We do need to tread very carefully."
Make sure that this is your mantra!

1 INTRODUCTION

There have been several books produced on the subject of building fuel-burning kilns. Many of them assume that the reader wishes to build a fairly large kiln, requiring a reasonable sized workforce to construct, and possibly a team of several people to fire. This approach ignores the large number of people who wish to build a kiln of moderate size in their own backyard or garden, able to be built and fired by one or maybe two people. It is towards these people; the small scale potters/builders, that my efforts are directed. Perhaps selfishly I have always wanted to plough my own furrow, and for me this approach particularly applies to this subject.

I feel that the only way to achieve a rapport with the tools and equipment that one uses is to be fully involved in their construction and eventual use. After all, we are all aware of the awful effects of 'committee design', and this applies to both building and firing kilns.

Over the years I have been involved with many different sorts of fuel burning kilns, starting with gas, which I was involved with right at the beginning of my career. I would probably have stayed in that simple groove had I not, by accident, become involved in a

BBC2 TV project, reconstructing an Iron Age Village. As the 'pottery expert', I had to help the inhabitants find a way of firing the pots they were making for everyday use, and so I was pitched headfirst into the, then mainly unexplored, mysteries of primitive firing. By the end of the project I was hooked and have spent the subsequent years exploring small scale effective firing techniques.

The kilns that I will be describing here are to be looked upon as a starting point for your own journey. Building and then modifying these projects to suit your own needs is one approach, but perhaps it is better to read and observe, and then, coming to your own conclusions, build something which is perhaps radically different. If at that the end of all this, you come to the conclusion that building a good kiln is not rocket science, but something anyone can do, then I will have achieved my objective.

3 A BIT OF HISTORY

The Double Cross-Draught Kiln

I have always known this type of kiln as a 'Philosopher's Kiln', as firing it is a comparatively relaxed affair, allowing time for observation, discussion, and enjoyment of the process.

This project began from a design more normally associated with Raku kilns. The utter simplicity of it is its greatest strength, and lends it to considerable personal modification. This was first assembled by a group of us at one of the Playing With Fire weekend courses I ran with Lexa Lawrance, using common house bricks, and was christened the '40 minute kiln' because that was exactly how long it took 5 of us to build it. This first incarnation (above) had far too small a firebox (10.12 cu ft, 7.59 cu ft pot chamber), and consequently got very choked very quickly.

We persevered with the firing however, and although we never got an indicated temperature above 950 degrees Centigrade, we found on opening it that we had obtained heatwork far in excess of that, which was very encouraging. The next version (right) which I built, was a much bigger effort all round, with the firebox almost half as big again (13.78 cu ft, with a 11.48 cu ft pot chamber), and although it fired very well, there were still some problems with choking. One other version with these proportions was built in Gloucestershire. This one incorporated 5 mouseholes, 3 on one side and 2 on the other, the idea being to promote the burning of the embers. This was an improvement, but I felt the firebox was still too small. The next version was built in a friend's garden, her husband having (wisely) given her a pile of bricks for Christmas. As we had fewer bricks to play with than normal, this version was shorter overall, but much deeper in the firebox. The proportions were: firebox 18.28 cu ft, pot chamber 7.59 cu ft. This kiln turned out to have almost ideal proportions; it fired easily and economically, and I found the depth of the pot chamber could be increased if need be without compromising its performance.

During 2003/4 this kiln was developed further still; initially in September 2003 with the addition of a metal chimney. This version was constructed, fired, and dismantled for a two day festival called Potfest in Frome, Somerset, UK, and the addition of a metal chimney reduced the building time. With 5 volunteers and myself it was built in 3 hours, and prepared and packed with bisque in 2 hours. We started firing at 14.40, and by 22.00 had cone 12 down and all shut down and sealed.

The results were excellent and all the participants had good pots out of it.

This kiln was rebuilt on the car park at Bath Potters Supplies, Radstock, Nr. Bath, UK, but with further important modifications; the addition of a perforated floor to the firebox, the closing of what had been the primary air opening at the front, and the removal of the mouseholes on either side. This meant that all the air had to come into the firebox through the floor and consequently through the embers promoting much better combustion of them and as a result greater pre-heating potential.

I used to think that I had got about as far as I could go with this kiln, WRONG! There is a lot of life left in this design, and as recent experience has shown me, lots of room for improvement and/or modification.

4 CONSTRUCTION

On this page, rather than give detailed step by step instructions, I have chosen to illustrate various stages in the building of this sort of kiln, showing variations of each type, with comments alongside.

Here are the beginnings of two versions of the same basic form. The top one employs 2 mouseholes on each side for secondary air to enter, primary air coming in through the ground level hole in the front. In the lower picture the firebox floor is made up of perforated bricks which is the only entry for air. Although there is the same hole at the front of this kiln, it is purely for post firing cleaning out, and is blocked up during firing.

The advantage of the perforated floor is that it positively encourages combustion of the embers over the entire floor thereby giving much better pre heating and consequently even better fuel economy. The 2 inner lines of bricks supporting the floor are also perforated to encourage air cross flow. The outer lines are plain house bricks. It's worth noting that the mouseholes are on one side, and the primary air entry at the front.

Here you can see the 3 channels which are the primary air entries in this design. The channels extend right through to the other end to provide enough for full combustion (see the notes on proportions at the end of this section). During firing one or more entries can be closed at either end to help vary the atmosphere inside.

The upper hole here is for stoking. The lintel is made from thick kiln shelf. I have used cast fire brick pieces before, but they lack strength and are short lived.

On the subject of stoking, one problem with a long firebox is that fuel needs to be thrown to the back in the latter stages of a firing. This has a punishing effect on the back wall, and has led in the past to bricks being knocked out of it during a firing. The solution is an inner replaceable loose brick wall which I call the "thump wall", just visible on the right (marked with the arrow).

Note also the ends of the two fire bars protruding from the wall on the right. The theory behind this is explained in the chapter on firing.

This has now reached the stage where the firebox is complete and the pot chamber and base of the chimney can be built. Notice that the last layer of bricks has been corbelled in to support the pot chamber base shelves. Notice also the gap at the end of the shelves to allow fire entry from the firebox. In this case it is about nine inches deep and the width of the kiln. As you will have also seen, the pot chamber base shelves are quite thick. This is needed to provide strong support for the wares packed in it, and also to give some degree of insulation as heat can be rapidly lost downwards. In some builds I have done the only shelves available were Silicon Carbide which are very thin, therefore it was necessary to make up a sandwich of two layers of shelves with Ceramic Fibre in between to achieve the required insulation.

The pot chamber and base of the chimney are now started, and you can see the two support bricks for the chamber side of the chimney. Unless you can use pre-fired and shrunk bricks for this, spacers will need to be inserted after the first firing to level things out again, as their shrinkage is considerable. The mug of coffee is not part of the kiln, but it is of course an essential part of the process!

So here we are with the kiln virtually finished and the chimney built. The top one, built of brick, has the advantage that its height can be adjusted up or down during the firing while you fine tune its performance. In fact all the chimneys are approximately the same height and internal diameter/dimensions, these were originally arrived at more by happy accident than careful calculation! However in "Additional Information" at the end of this chapter their proportions are explained. The advantage of the removable chimney is that it is much easier to wrap the whole kiln up against the elements without it in place.

It is now important to tie the whole structure up with angle iron at all corners bound together with fencing wire and barrel tensioners (turnbuckles). I have found it useful to insert half sections of steel tubing on the corners to ease the stretching process of the fencing wire (see the drawing below). You will see two tensioners (turnbuckles) on the left-hand side of the kiln, roughly in the middle

Steve Mills

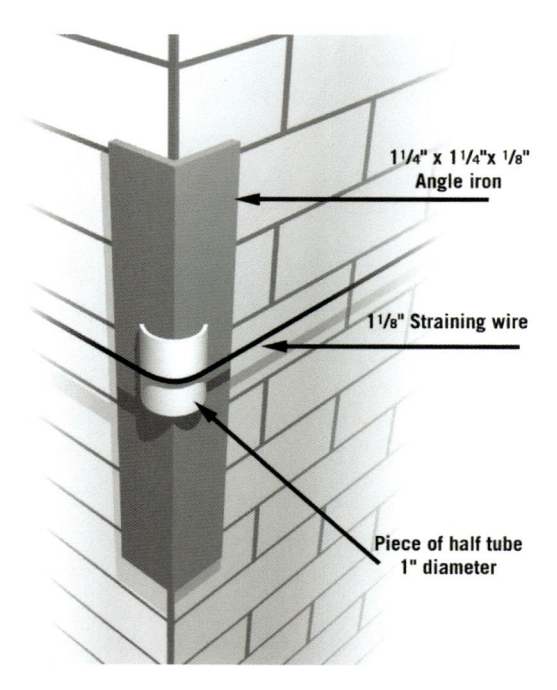

1¼" x 1¼" x ⅛" Angle iron

1⅛" Straining wire

Piece of half tube 1" diameter

5 DOOR CONSTRUCTION

There are as many solutions to how you approach making a firebox door as there are days in a year! The easy solution is an old kiln shelf held in place with a piece of metal and lowered onto a brick column when stoking (see below left). The problem with that is it is very easy to drop it in the flurry of stoking, and they don't bounce! The solution I have arrived at with the latest build involves:

- 4 bits of angle iron

- 3 threaded rods

- 2 gate hinge pins

- 2 bits of tube

- 4 insulating fire bricks

The fire bricks have slots cut in them for the angle iron to sit in, and the hinge pins just go through two plain holes in the ends of the angle iron. A simple catch could be made to hold it shut. This one stays shut without needing one, more by luck than intent.

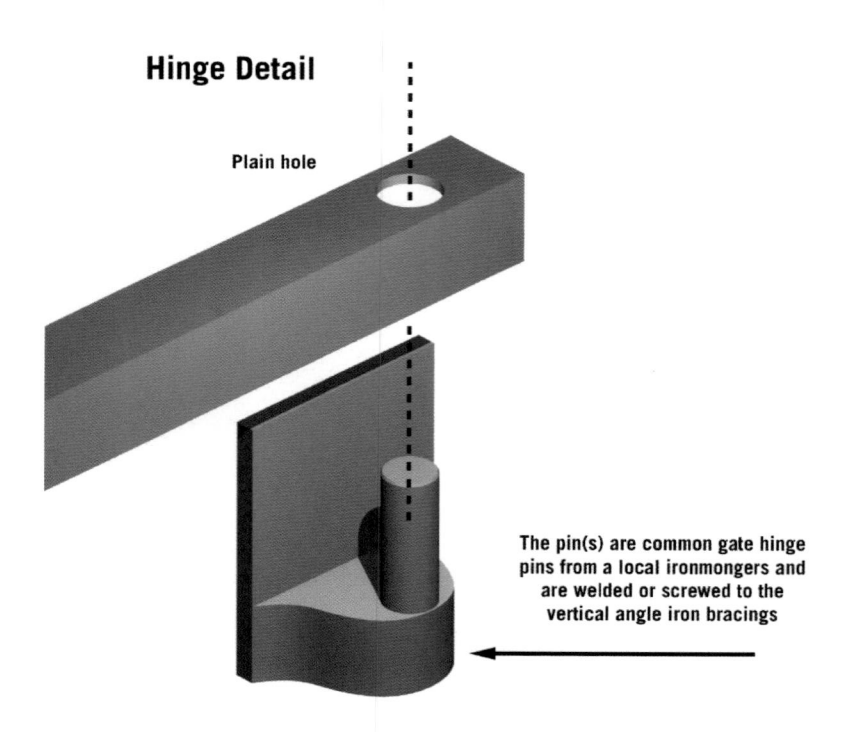

Hinge Detail

Plain hole

The pin(s) are common gate hinge pins from a local ironmongers and are welded or screwed to the vertical angle iron bracings

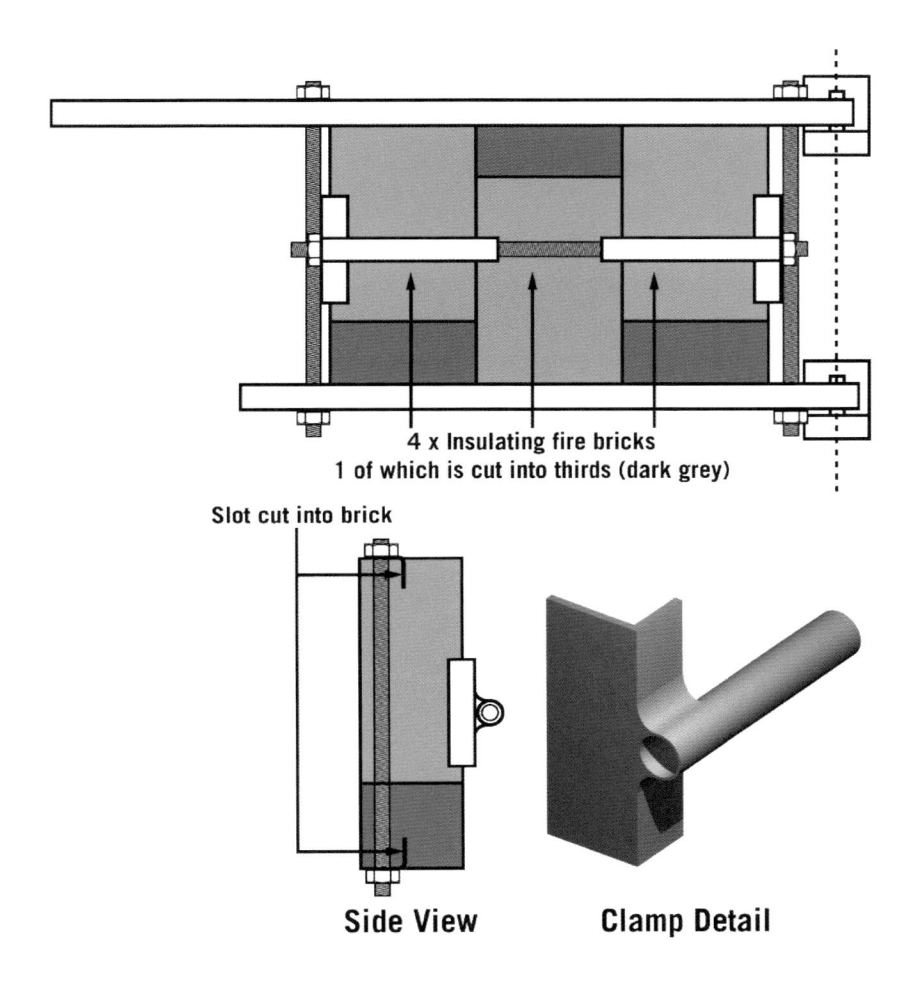

4 x Insulating fire bricks
1 of which is cut into thirds (dark grey)

Slot cut into brick

Side View   Clamp Detail

The last thing I do is to make up a mixture of equal parts of scrap clay, sand, and sawdust. Initially this is used to fill up any cracks or unevenness in the joints between the bricks. It can also be used as an insulating layer on the outside of the kiln. You can see some evidence of its use in the last picture on the right. I also use it as a seal between the pot chamber and the thick shelves that make up its lid.

The cover for the pot chamber is as you can see made up with kiln shelves. As this is not load bearing almost any refractory slab able to take high temperatures can be used, though if they are thin, some form of insulation should be added. The cheapest is a thick layer of equal parts of clay, sand, and sawdust. The easiest is Ceramic Fibre, preferably the Body Soluble type, though you should always wear a respirator and gloves when handling Fibre what ever type it is!

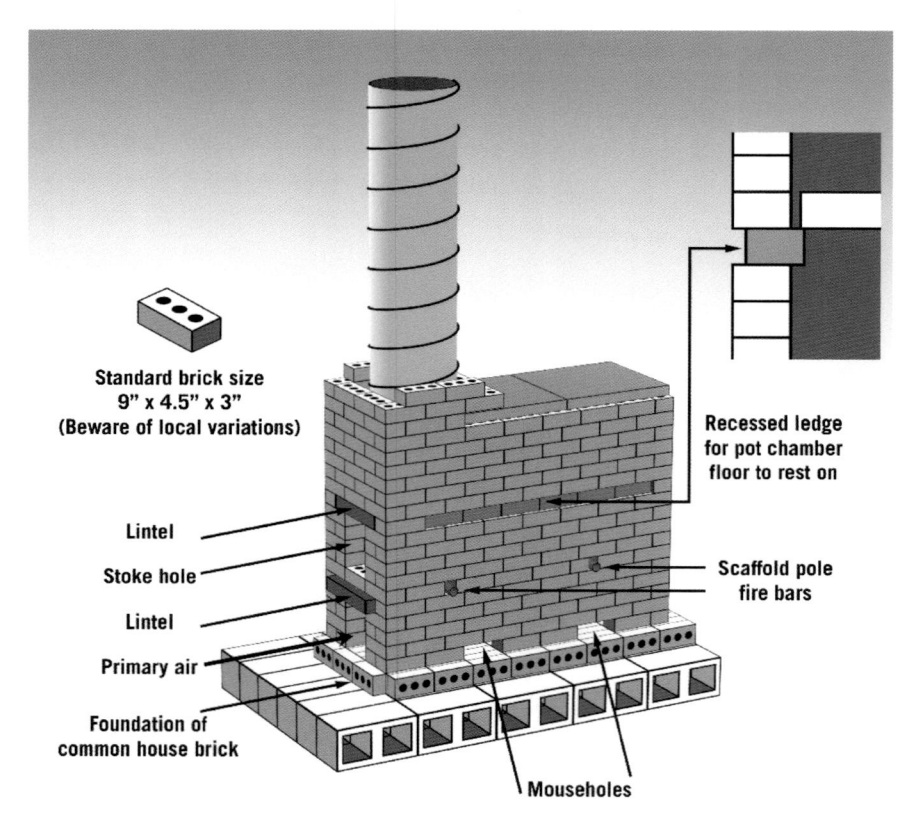

**Standard brick size
9" x 4.5" x 3"
(Beware of local variations)**

Recessed ledge for pot chamber floor to rest on

Lintel
Stoke hole
Lintel
Primary air
Foundation of common house brick

Scaffold pole fire bars

Mouseholes

It is a good bet that if you can find a buff coloured house brick, then it will fire to a much higher temperature than common red brick will. This is certainly the case where I live near Bristol in the UK. Just north of that city there are extensive clay fields of a highly refractory clay from which are made the bricks which I use for my kilns. They are not as heavy and dense as hard fire brick, but they are very cheap and work very well for me thank you!

Note: In nearly all the kilns of this type I have built I have used brick locally available to me, the dimensions of which are 9 X 4½ X 3 inches. All the plans etc. in this book are based on these measurements. This does not necessarily apply where you are, as I found out (the hard way) recently when building one of these in a different part of the UK. Here, some of the local brick I used were smaller, not by much, but enough to alter the basic proportions of the kiln the wrong way, and I noticed a bit late in the day! So let your watchword be: "Beware of local variations!"

Steve Mills

This page is left mysteriously blank

6 ADDITIONAL INFORMATION

Although the design of this kiln was not calculated in this fashion, examination of its proportions will show that it conforms to several of the principles laid down by Fred Olsen in his excellent kiln book. In chapter 3: Principles of Design - Principal 3 the ground rule for the grate/flue areas for wood fired kilns is a ratio of 10 to 1; the area of the grate being ten times that of the area of the flue, however he modifies this rule to 7 to 1 as a result of experience as this makes the kiln much easier to fire: "it allows for a more forgiving firing technique, fires faster when needed, adjusts for altitude, and allows for adjustability in altering flues, chimney height and dampering". Thus the grate area of this kiln is 1134 square inches which gives us a flue area of 162. In Principle 6 he asserts "for natural draft kilns there should be three feet of chimney to every foot of downward pull, plus 1 foot of chimney to every three feet of horizontal pull". In this kiln we have approximately 18 inches of downward pull which gives us 4 foot 6 inches of flue, and 45 inches of horizontal pull which theoretically adds another 15 inches. Since the calculation for height of chimney starts at the point at which the gases leave the pot chamber you can see that the proportions are just about right at a total of 6 feet. Where there is some deviation from Fred's Principles is in the latest incarnation of this kiln. Going back to Principal 3 he states that the inlet and exit areas should be identical, in this case 162 inches

Horizontal pull →

Downward pull ↓

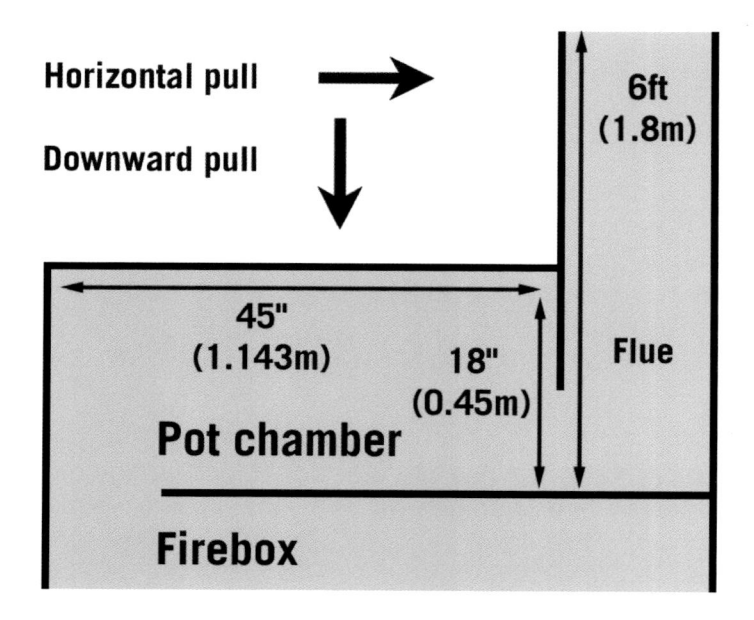

```
         45"
      (1.143m)        18"        Flue    6ft
                    (0.45m)             (1.8m)
      Pot chamber

      Firebox
```

In the case of the Potfest and previous kilns, that balance was correct as all primary air entered the kiln through a right sized hole just below the stoke hole. In the latest version where all primary air comes in through the firebox floor, the combined area of the three vents at either end of the kiln only totals 135 square inches. Nonetheless it fires very efficiently and does not seem to miss those 27 inches! However as the kiln is entirely constructed of dry laid bricks, with nary a spot of mortar or any other joint sealant, I suspect that the missing 27 inches are more than compensated for by a lot of small gaps in the brickwork!

You may notice in all variations in this kiln, that there is no damper. It was accidentally omitted in the first version, but wasn't missed, and I have rarely found the need for it since. Any adjustment needed such as reduction, or slowing down the firing process can be very effectively achieved by controlling the primary air and or by under or over stoking. Sealing the kiln after the firing is done by closing off the primary air and putting a lid on the chimney. In the case of a metal chimney this is removed first and the base is sealed with a spare kiln shelf.

7 MATERIALS AND TOOLS LIST

Materials

- 27 hollow concrete blocks (see note at end of list)
- 360 fire bricks or similar
- 56 perforated bricks (firebox floor)
- 20 common house bricks
- 4 pieces angle iron 51 by 1 ½ inches (130 by 3.8 cm)
- 2 pieces thick kiln shelf 12 by 6 by 2 inches (30 by 15 by 5 cm) or fairly close to those dimensions, plus odd scraps of kiln shelf for packing out
- 1 coil medium grade galvanised fencing wire
- 4 galvanised turnbuckles
- 4 pieces 2 by 1 inch tube (10 by 5 cm), halved 8 total
- 2 pieces heavy duty steel scaffold tube 30 inches long (76 cm)
- 6 heavy duty kiln shelves 18 by 18 by 2 inches (45 by 45 by 5 cm)
- 1 length of steel tube (preferably stainless) 48 by 14 inches (122 by 35 cm). Flattened into an oval approximately 9 inches (23 cm) wide on its narrowest dimension for the chimney
- Scrap clay
- Sand
- Sawdust

Materials for firebox door

- 4 pieces of angle iron, one the same length as the width of the kiln, the other 2/3 of that, and 2
- pieces the height of the firebox door hole plus about 2 inches (5 cm)
- 3 threaded rods, 1 X 12 inches (30 cm) long the other 2 about 15 inches (47cm) long
- 2 gate hinge pins
- 2 bits of tube
- 4 insulating fire bricks

The two pieces of tube are welded to the two shortest lengths of angle iron. This is the only bit of welding involved in the making of this kiln.

Note: Hollow concrete blocks make sense as the foundation for a kiln; any rising moisture from the ground beneath is dispersed by airflow through them, and should the kiln be built on a vulnerable surface such as Tarmac they prevent that from degradation through heat!

These are the tools that I have found useful while building this sort of kiln.

Tools

- Heavy Duty Gloves
- Rubber Mallet
- Bolster Chisel
- Lump hammer (4 pound)
- Angle Grinder and stone cutting Blades
- Spirit Level
- Two pairs strong Pliers
- Heavy duty Wire Cutters
- 48 x 2 x 2 inch piece of Straight Timber (120 cm x 5cm x 5cm)
- 3 litres thick Batt Wash
- A coarse Brush

8 KILN PLANS

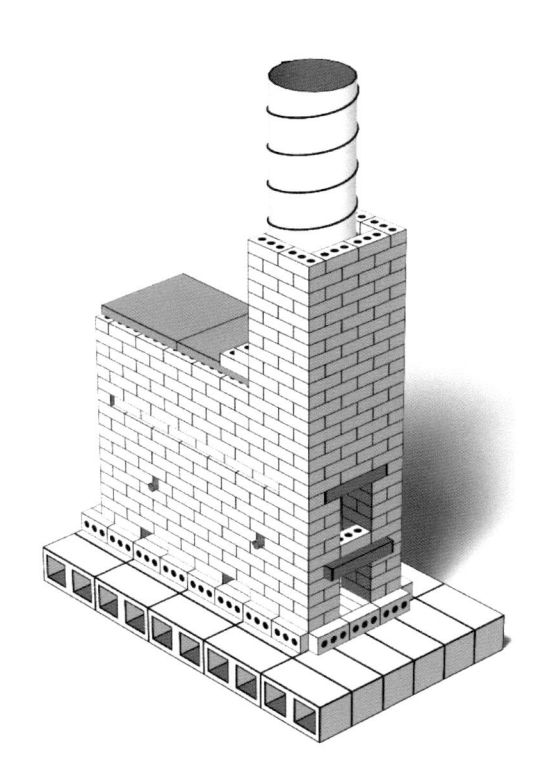

Steve Mills

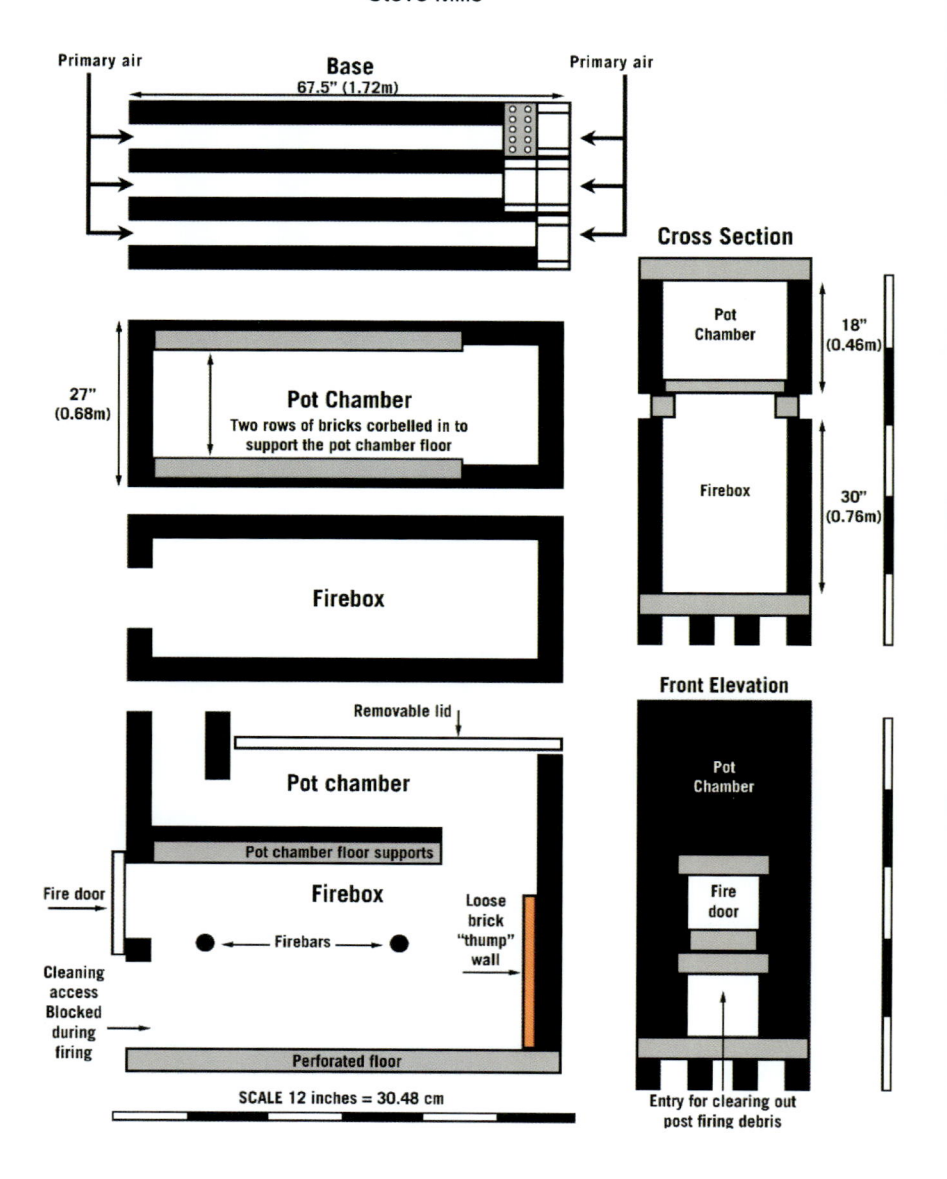

Base
67.5" (1.72m)

Primary air → ← Primary air

Pot Chamber
27" (0.68m)

Two rows of bricks corbelled in to support the pot chamber floor

Firebox

Cross Section

Pot Chamber — 18" (0.46m)

Firebox — 30" (0.76m)

Removable lid

Pot chamber

Pot chamber floor supports

Fire door

Firebox

Firebars

Loose brick "thump" wall

Cleaning access Blocked during firing →

Perforated floor

SCALE 12 inches = 30.48 cm

Front Elevation

Pot Chamber

Fire door

Entry for clearing out post firing debris

Backyard Kilns

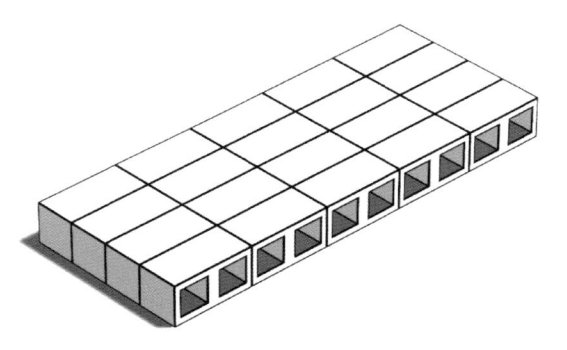

Stage 1

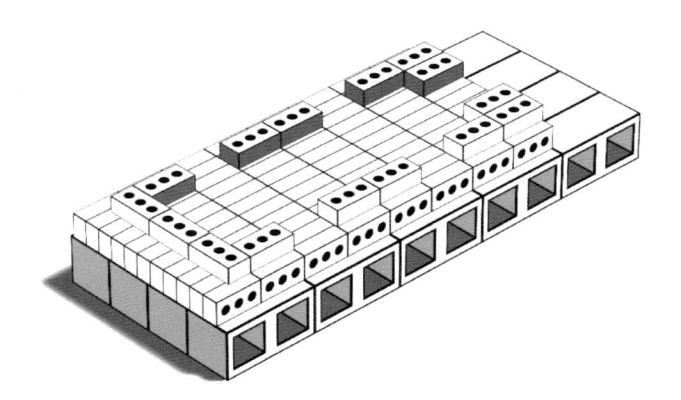

Stage2

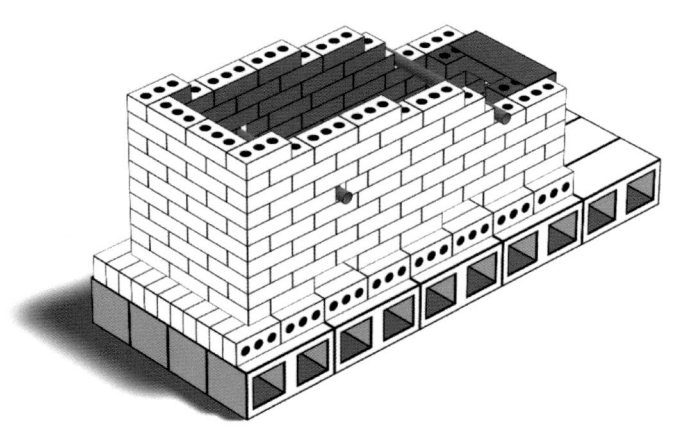

Stage 3

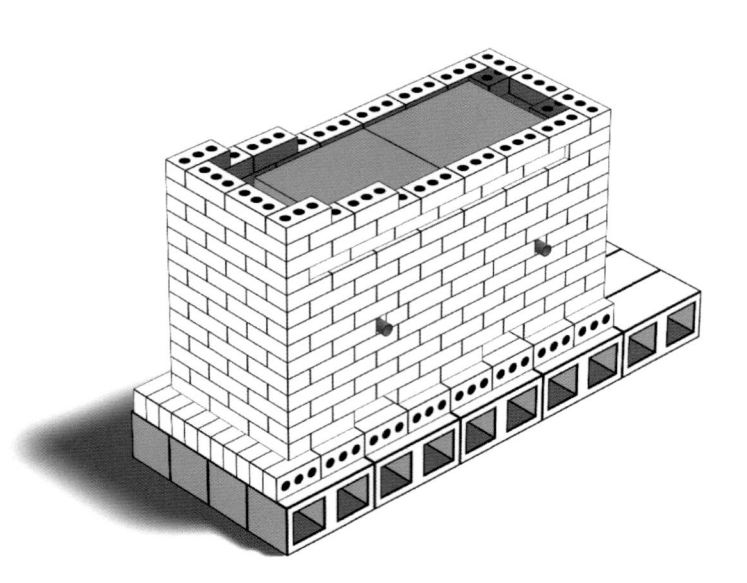

Stage 4

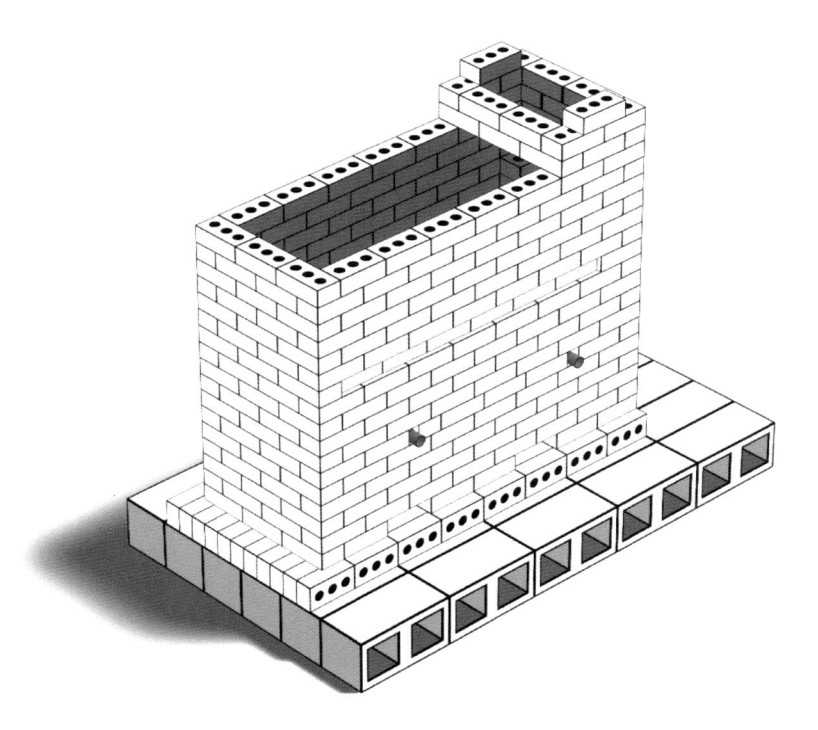

Stage 5

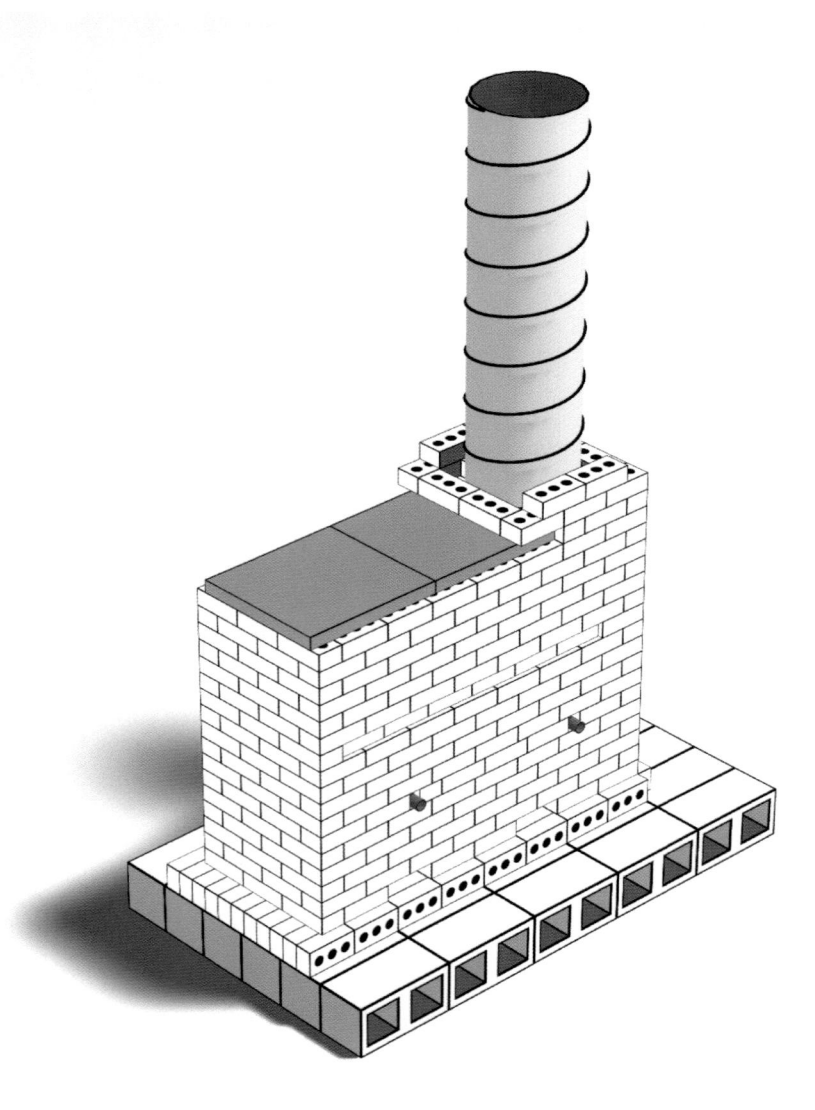

Stage 6

9 THE FIRING AND FIREBOX DESIGN

In any fuel burning kiln, there is one overriding rule and that is; the hotter the firebox the more efficient and effective the firing. To achieve this end there have been many differing approaches, but in the end they all boil down to one of two designs. These two basic types are the standard firebox, and the Bourry box.

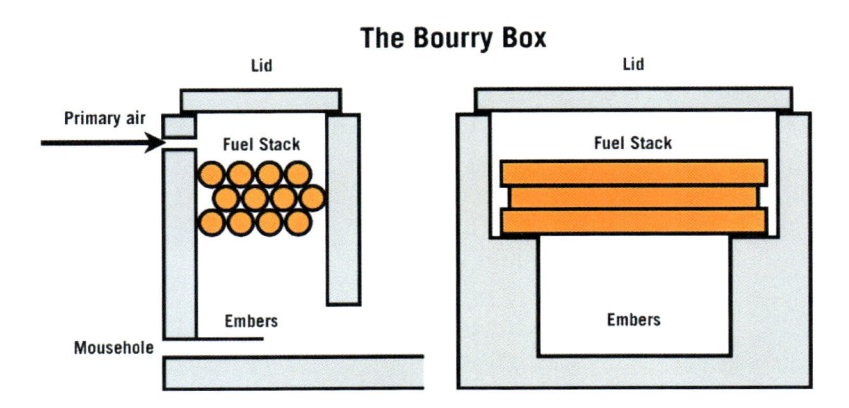

The Bourry Box

In the former you have a longish firebox leading into the pot chamber, divided horizontally by a row of fire bars. The fuel is loaded onto the bars, and the space below forms the ash pit. In its simplest form, this is basically an inefficient design.

There is too much space beneath the bars, allowing cold air to enter the kiln, even with a good bed of embers, and with the air being drawn in over them, it will have relatively little effect on the fuel above it which makes retaining heat in that area very difficult. Also because the fire bars are in a horizontal plane leading to the pot chamber, fuel resting on them cannot burn efficiently because the flames are travelling along its length and preventing air from reaching the rest of it.

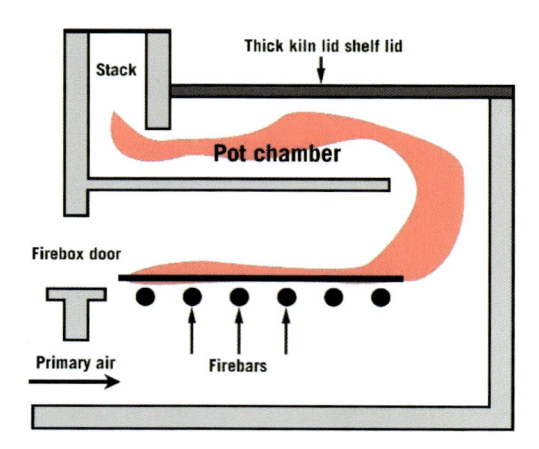

The Bourry box design is much more efficient, but it does demand that all the fuel used is of the same length, there is little allowance for variation. As this kiln is designed to use waste, recycled, or scrap timber for fuel, what you can get is what you use, there is little choice.

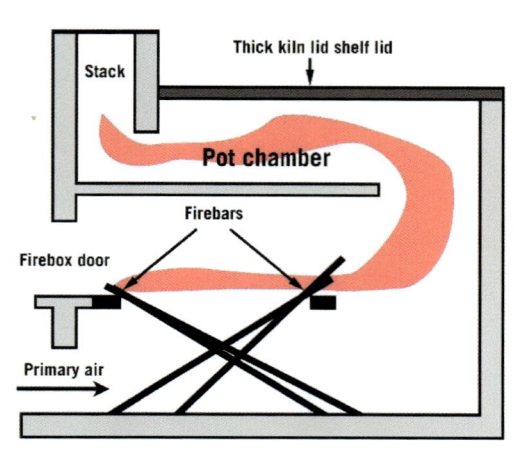

To overcome these two problems I use my own version of the standard firebox in the kilns I build. Instead of a row of fire bars I have just two, the first a quarter of the way into the box, and the second the same distance from the other end of the firebox. With this arrangement fuel is thrown in so that it either tilts forwards off the front bar, or tilts back from the back bar. With the fuel tilted at an angle to the direction of air flow, air reaches it comfortably, and is prevented from going through the firebox without touching anything because the fuel is in the way. Consequently the fuel is able to get the proper pre-heat from the embers, and also burns along a broad front without obstruction. This means optimal release of heat from a small quantity of fuel.

In the case of a long narrow firebox such as in a small low ceilinged Anagama or tube kiln, where you have a firebox which is wide rather than deep, the technique is to angle the fuel across it, almost from side to side, to create the same broad front of flames. Again this achieves the same aim of maximising the effective combustion of a given quantity of fuel.

With any firing there is an initial warming up period, gently building heat within the entire structure. For this I tend to use largish lumps of timber which burn steadily and unspectacularly. Once warmed through, I can start using thinner timber, always in small quantities, gradually increasing the rate of temperature rise until I see evidence of red heat in the pot chamber. At this point I change to very thin timber in small quantities, stoking quite frequently, the objective being to raise the firebox temperature to the point where the fuel explodes into flame rather than "catching fire".

Note: At all times it is essential to monitor the amount of fuel that is fed into the firebox. Too much and you get great clouds of smoke, a clear indication that there is too much in there and it cannot burn properly. There is always an initial burst of smoke as you stoke, but if you've got your quantities right this should clear relatively quickly be followed by a short period of cleaner burning followed by an absolutely clean burn. When you get to this point open the door and check how much there is left unburnt if any, maybe throw one or perhaps two small bits in, or maybe not, either way be watchful and try to guess what the kiln needs.

Take notes if necessary, and if you can employ a pyrometer and thermocouple to aid your deductions so much the better. You will notice that the temperature fluctuates quite strongly; this is normal, what you are aiming to do is to get the end point temperature when you have to re-stoke a little bit higher each time, and maintain or exceed it after the next stoke. This won't always work; the condition of the fuel has an enormous bearing on the efficiency of the firing. Fuel must be very dry, and well seasoned to perform properly. This is one of the advantages of using scrap timber such as building site reclaim, palettes, old floorboards etc. is that you know they are seasoned, and all you have to do is make sure they are thoroughly dry. Damp timber won't burn properly, resulting in an increasing ember bed, which instead of burning efficiently eventually clogs the firebox and can stagnate the firing. The partial answer is to rake out the excess and introduce really dry fuel into the firebox. The real answer is to be prepared with lots of really dry wood, stacked so that it can continue to dry (open stacking) in a covered store. But then if you are going down this wood firing road you will realize that a proper wood store is as important as the kiln.

Not too little	Not too much	But just right!

This may sound a bit "cosmic", but I have always maintained that the kiln will tell you what it wants, all you have to do is learn the language, and the old kiln firing saw "more is less" applies in full measure at all times.

10 CONSTRUCTION MODIFICATIONS SUPPLEMENT: BUILDING IN A DAMPER

I decided to build a damper into later variations of this kiln, largely because it simplified the process of shutting it down at the end of the firing. I have never felt the need to use it to control atmosphere.

The pictures here are from an earthenware firing version, and have been used because they are the clearest illustrations I have of the "mechanics" of it. The clamps are simple W pieces made up by welding two bits of angle iron together thus:

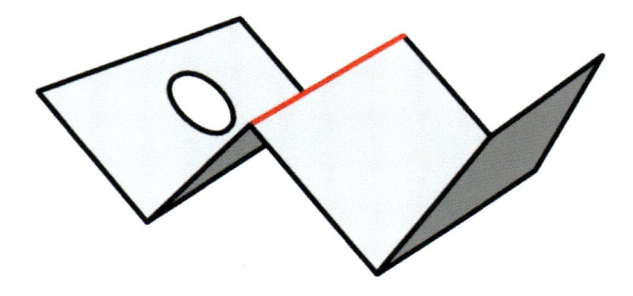

The rods holding them together are obtainable from any Builder's Merchants or DIY Store. I have used kiln shelving of two different thicknesses; the thinner for the damper plate, the other cut into strips to make the "casing" around it.

I have positioned the damper so that the plate projects over the kiln body, as any other placement means it is at exactly the right height for kiln stokers to crack their heads on it!!

SUPPLEMENT: AN ALTERNATIVE DOOR

The chief advantage of this alternative is that when opened, hot face of the door is directed away from the operator. Hopefully the accompanying diagram is self-explanatory.

The U shaped frame the door is suspended in is made from square section tube.

The door frame is made from angle iron, with four small pieces of the same material as retainers to keep the contents in place.

I have not shown any means for keeping the door shut, as that will depend on "local conditions"! I suggest that the clips retain only the backing board (B) in place, and that the fibre (A) is cemented on top of that to prevent heat degradation (C)

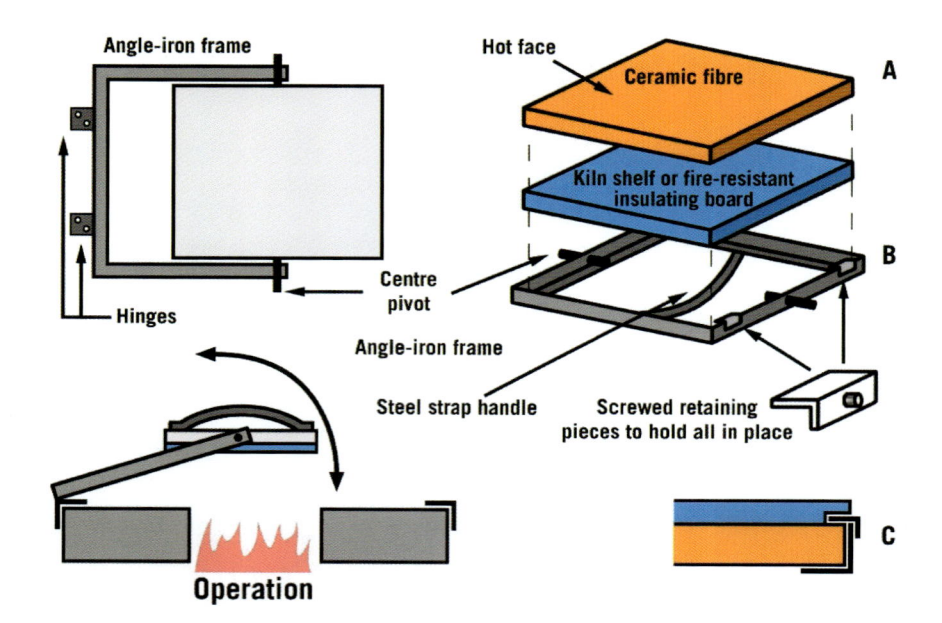

Backyard Kilns

11 PHOTOS

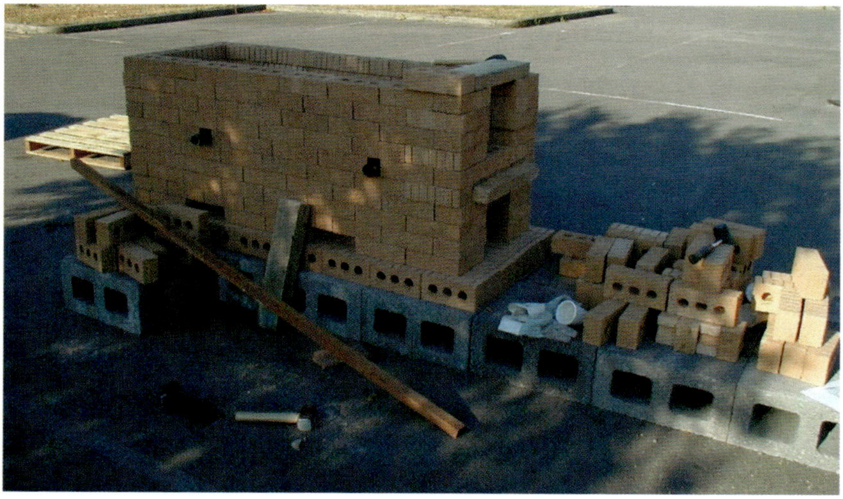

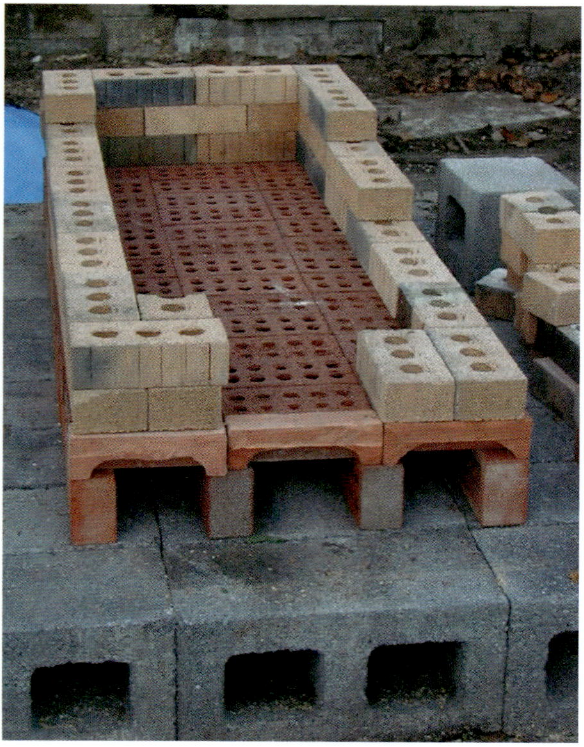

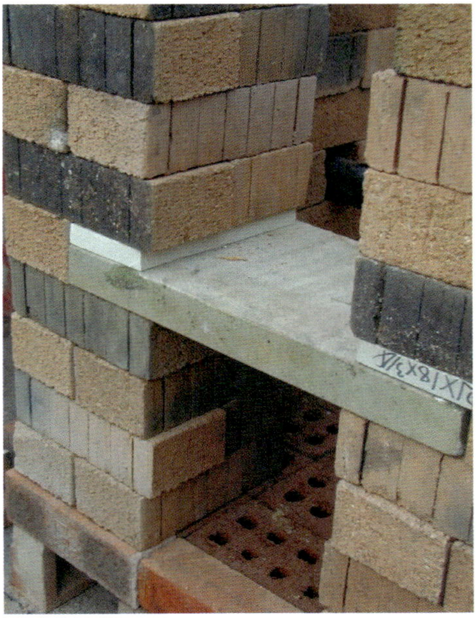

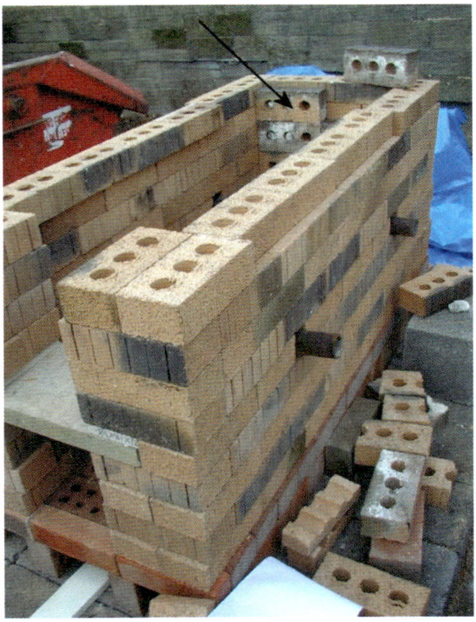

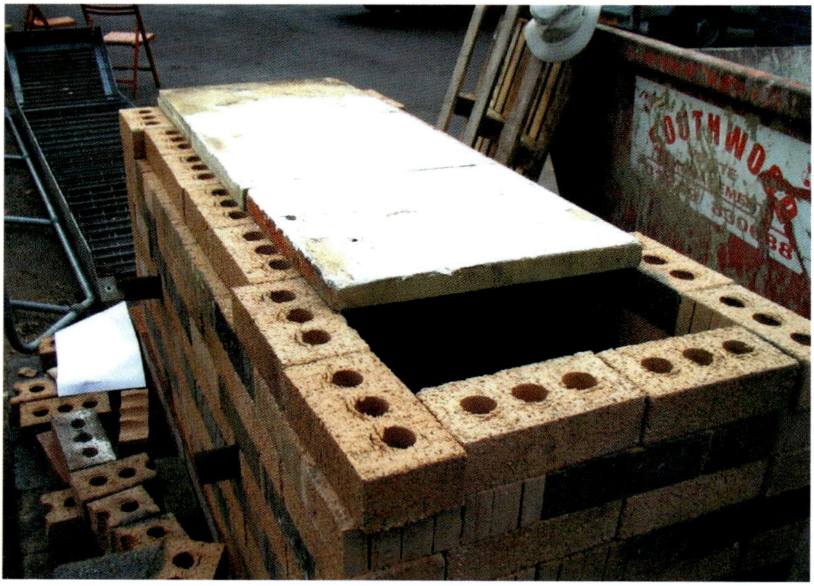

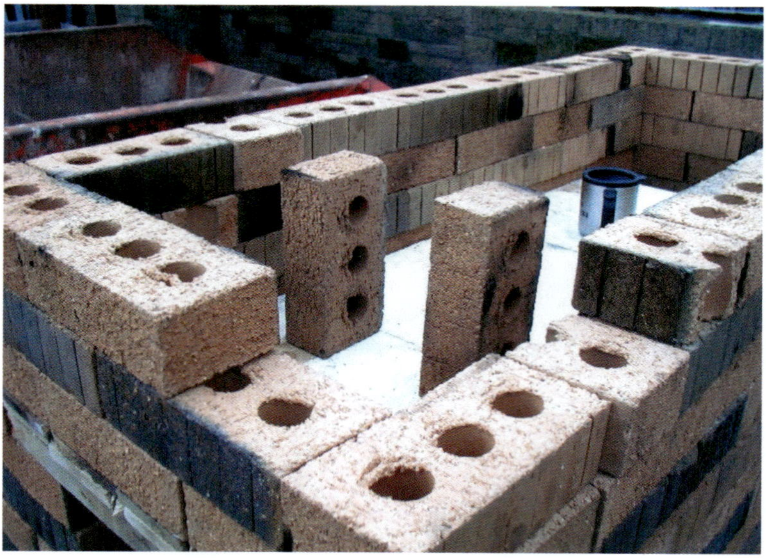

Backyard Kilns

Steve Mills

Like I said: they don't bounce!

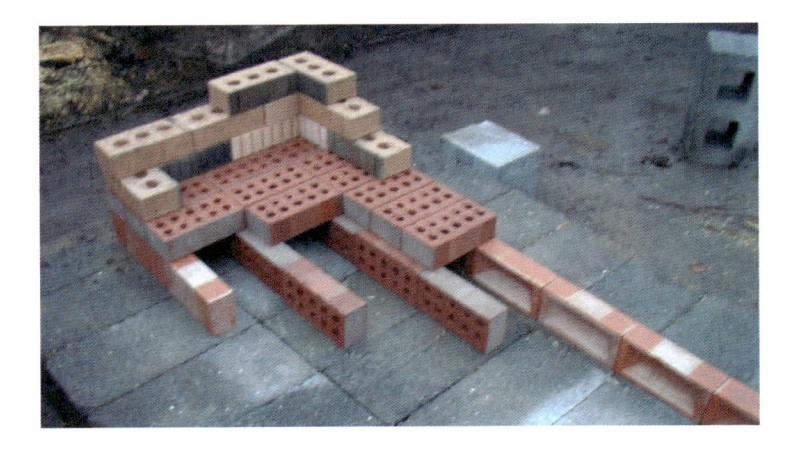

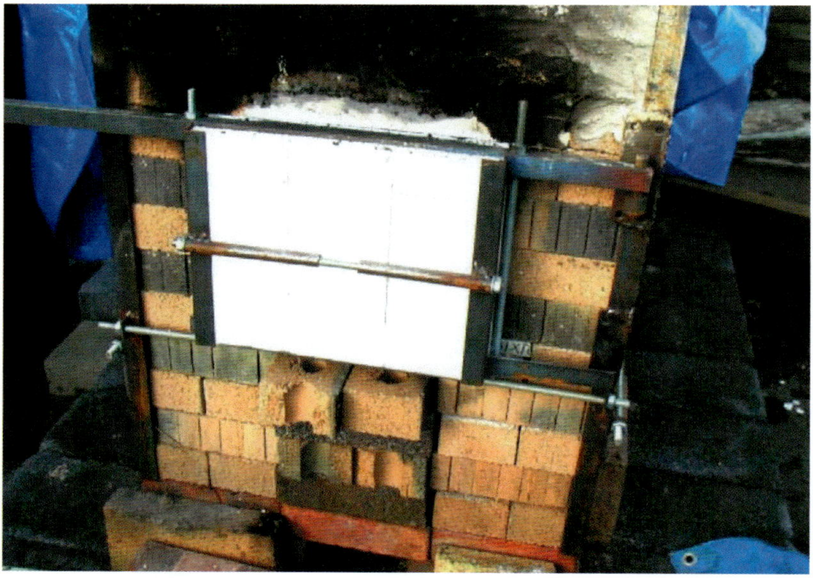

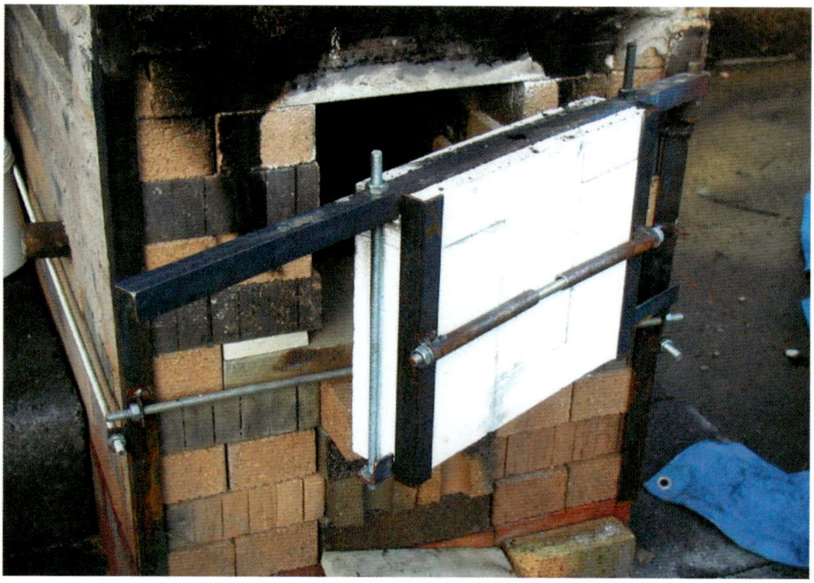

Backyard Kilns

Steve Mills

Bath Potter's Supplies
Suppliers of raw materials, tools, kilns, glazes, clays and casting slips.
http://www.bathpotters.co.uk/

Craft Fair
Details of crafters, suppliers, craft guilds, organisations and forthcoming craft events.
http://www.craft-fair.co.uk/

Top Pot Supplies
Family run mail order pottery supply business.
http://www.toppotsupplies.co.uk/

Northern Kilns
Range of hobbyist and industrial kilns.
http://www.northernkilns.com/

Comartie Kilns
Commercial and industrial kiln design and builders.
http://www.cromartie.co.uk/

Potfest
Pottery markets in the UK, putting Public and Potters together..
http://www.potfest.co.uk/

Digital Fire
Ceramic chemistry software specialists.
http://www.digitalfire.com/

Wali Hawes
An Unconfined potter, sideways thinker and pyromantic
http://www.walihawes.com/

Steve Mills
The author's website
http://stevemillsmudslinger.weebly.com/

WWW.MUDSLINGER.ME.UK

Addendum

I was asked by Steve to update his drawings and this guide with the hope that it would replace the existing version of Backyard Kilns distributed from his website on CD. He was very keen to create an e-book version and for me to include stage by stage kiln building illustrations; much like the ones you get with plastic bricks. Sadly Steve was unable to do any of this. However, we think it fitting that Backyard Kilns be part of his legacy, accessible to all, for free. That's "free" as in beer.

This is the printed version of that e-book, and for obvious reasons it isn't available for free. But, if you are going to have a legacy it'd be quite nice to a have one that can sit on a shelf and gather dust at some point. Cheers, Steve. - CK

If you wish to reproduce any part of this, you may do so provided you fully acknowledge its origin and its Author together with what you choose to reproduce.

ABOUT THE AUTHOR

Steve Mills, who has died at the age of 78, was a Bath potter whose enthusiasm and encyclopedic knowledge of his craft took him around the world building his own design of kilns in the ten years since he retired from a business supplying pottery materials.

Steve Mills' designs for wood-fired kilns are now operating on four continents. All have been constructed and fired by one person in a day, a simple, efficient solution he was happy to share freely. He was internationally recognised as an authority on kiln construction and a range of pottery glazes he made from wood ash.

Printed in Great Britain
by Amazon